ON THE OTHER SIDE
OF MY DREAM

KEN MOORMAN

DEDICATION

This book is dedicated to my wife, Detra. Thank you for your support. I would not have a Jirani story to tell without you. To my beautiful mother Joyce for teaching me how to love and to my father for teaching me the importance of working hard for the things you want and to always treat everyone with respect. To Mom Shubbie for always encouraging me to never give up on pursuing my dreams. To Aunt Betty and Big Mot for your love and always being there for me. Lastly, I dedicate this book to my beautiful and amazing children: Chuck, Buto, and Kenadi. I want to share parts of my life with you that will help you in your life journey. I pray that this book will continue to encourage you to follow your dreams. I love you all so much.

TABLE OF CONTENTS

ACKNOWLEDGMENTS

Writing a book was very challenging, but I found the process to be very therapeutic and healing for me. None of this would have been possible without my Cousin Sabu. Thank you for encouraging me to write this book and helping me to the finish line. No one accomplishes anything alone. Along my journey I have had so many people encourage and inspire me to use all of my gifts and to follow my dreams. There are too many of you to mention, but you know who you are, and I thank you from the bottom of my heart! Special thanks to Jesse for your support and for believing in me and the vision to love on our community through coffee and the arts!

INTRODUCTION

ARE YOU A CARROT, AN EGG, OR A COFFEE BEAN?

I found this story on a blog at AlanWongs.com. Alan runs a restaurant in Honolulu, Hawaii. Physically, he and I couldn't be farther apart. But after reading this story, I realize that spiritually, we're closer than I'd have thought possible.

This a humbling story about perspective, adversity, and how you view the things that are happening in your life. He says he shared it with his staff, and I want to share it with you.

The story goes like this:

A young woman went to her mother and told her about her life and how things were so hard for her. She did not know how she was going to make it. She wanted to give up. She was tired of fighting and struggling. It seemed like every time one problem was solved, a new one arose.

Her mother said nothing but took her to the kitchen. She filled three pots with water. In the first she placed carrots, in the second she placed eggs, and in the last she placed ground coffee beans.

She let them sit and boil for about twenty minutes without saying a word. Then she turned off the burners. She fished the carrots out and placed them in a bowl. She pulled the eggs out and placed them in a bowl. Then she ladled the coffee into a bowl.

Turning to her daughter, she said, "Tell me what you see."

"Carrots, eggs, and coffee," she replied.

She brought her daughter closer and asked her to feel the carrots. She did and noted that they were soft. She then asked her to take an egg and break it. After pulling off the shell, she observed the hard-boiled egg. Finally, she asked her to sip the coffee. The daughter smiled as she tasted its rich aroma.

The daughter then asked, "What's the point, mother?"

Her mother explained that each of these objects had faced the same adversity—boiling water— but each reacted differently.

The carrot went in strong, hard, and unrelenting.

However, after being subjected to the boiling water, it softened and became weak.

The egg had been fragile. Its thin outer shell had protected its liquid interior. But after the boiling water, the insides hardened.

But the ground coffee beans were unique. After they were in the boiling water, they had not changed, but had changed the water, the environment around them.

"Which are you?" she asked the daughter. "When adversity knocks on your door, how do you respond? Are you a carrot, an egg, or a coffee bean?"

Think of this: Which are you?

Are you the carrot that seems strong, but with pain and adversity, you wilt and become soft and lose your strength?

Are you the egg that starts with a soft heart, but changes and hardens with the heat? Do you have a fluid spirit, but after some trial—the death of a loved one, a break up, or a financial hardship, perhaps—will you harden and become stiff?

Or are you like the coffee bean? The bean actually changes the hot water, the very circumstance that brings the pain. When the water gets hot, it releases its fragrance and flavor. If you are like the bean, when things are at their worst, you get better and change the situation around you.

When the hours are the darkest and trials are their greatest, do you elevate to another level? In life, things happen around us and to us, but what matters is what happens within us.

How do you handle adversity? Are you a carrot, an egg, or a coffee bean?

THE JOURNEY OF A COFFEE BEAN

Coffee beans go through many processes before they're ready to be brewed. Once a coffee tree is planted, it takes three to five years before the cherries start to grow.

The cherry must go through several processes before the coffee bean inside is ready for consumption. First, coffee beans grow in small clusters because they are too small to be mechanically harvested, and machine picking can bruise and ruin the cherry. So workers must pick the cherries by hand. Once they're picked, they must be dried, often on a concrete slab in the hot sun. Too much sun and they become brittle and unusable. Too little sun and they mold and can't be used.

Once the beans are dried, then workers must sort through the cherries to get the best value. The selected cherries go through a process of pulping, which involves removing the skin from the cherry. Finally, inside the cherry is the coffee bean. But the harvest isn't over. The coffee bean is then pre-graded. After that, there's a fermentation process to remove the sweet film around the coffee bean. Next, there's underwater soaking, a final washing, and then a final grading of the coffee bean.

It takes a lot of steps to realize a coffee bean harvest.

Anything can happen along the way, and a lot of beans don't make it to a final grading, let alone to a cup of coffee. So what you see in your cup is more than "just a bean." It's a bean that survived an arduous seven to nine months on a coffee shrub, then the physical collection, the drying process, and the fermentation process. What you get from the coffee bean that makes it to a coffee shop, or a bag you buy, is a bean that's been through more than you'll ever see, and yet, at the end it's there to give you the hot, smooth flavor that can make your day, start your morning, connect you with friends, soothe you, comfort you, relax you, and energize you. Remember this the next time you sip a cup of coffee.

Dark roasted coffees are dark brown in color, like chocolate. Sometimes the beans are almost black. They have a sheen of oil on their surface, which is usually evident in the cup when the dark roast coffee is brewed. The coffee's origin flavors are eclipsed by the flavors of the roasting process. The coffee will generally have a bitter and smoky or even burnt taste. They should. They've been through the fire.

Water boils at 212 degrees. To reach the level of a dark roast, coffee beans are roasted to an internal temperature of 240°C (446°F)—about the end of the second crack—or beyond.

Coffee goes through two "cracks" when roasting. These are literally audible sounds the bean makes as it cracks open. A light to medium roast will finish somewhere between the two roasts.

Dark roasts will typically be roasted past a second

crack, so called because the moisture forms steam, and then pressure, that forces the beans to crack open. At the second crack the moisture will begin to evaporate. It is this magical process where the roaster must use all five senses to see, hear, smell, touch, and taste the moment when the coffee reaches a perfect profile, or becomes burnt and undrinkable.

At some point in the heat of the fire, the origin character of the coffee really doesn't matter much. All coffees will tend to taste the same (i.e. ashy and bitter). It is up to the roaster to navigate the variables of roasting to create the coffee people come to truly enjoy. God, I believe, is the expert roaster. He knows how much heat, how long, and how much the beans can take before they're ruined. Trust Him.

What I find most amazing is that each stage a coffee bean must go through is harder than the last. It is picked, graded, roasted, and finally ground. If you think about it, by the time it's ready to drink, it should be brittle, bitter, and undrinkable.

Before we can fully appreciate a finely-brewed cup of coffee, the coffee bean, once roasted in the fire, must then go through the grinding process. The purpose of grinding is to break down the roasted coffee bean to expose the interior of the bean and allow the right amount of oils and flavors to be extracted. Ground coffee has much more surface area than whole bean coffee, allowing water (the extraction agent) to make contact with more facets of the coffee when brewing. More surfaces means more flavor. The more the bean is ground down, the richer, more flavorful the coffee. Just when the bean thinks its life can't get any worse, the grind continues.

It doesn't matter if you are drinking drip coffee light or dark roast, a latte with or without flavored syrups, or cappuccino or a caramel macchiato; there is something to be said about that first sip without the lid on. When it's grown, dried, roasted, ground, then prepared correctly, that first taste of coffee is magical. It's such a satisfying experience that we coffee drinkers all understand the draw a cup of fresh coffee has. Am I right? A good sip of that first cup of coffee makes you excited—ready to journey to the last drop. The first sip of your first refill duplicates the aforementioned experience. Coffee is a culture, and those who understand it understand what it means to find a truly good cup of coffee.

Many people outside the harvest, roasting, and grinding culture don't understand the journey the humble coffee bean takes to reach their mug. They enjoy a good cup of coffee, but they can't appreciate it until they understand what it took to reach the end of its journey.

THE JIRANI STORY

I'm the owner and founder of the Jirani Coffeehouse in Old Town Manassas, Virginia. The coffeehouse was born on March 24, 2016. In Swahili, Jirani means "neighbor" or "neighborhood." I named the coffeehouse Jirani hoping that the shop would bring my neighborhood together—all races, all colors, all religions. I'm grateful to say that it's accomplished that and so much more.

My entrepreneurial journey was humbling and astounding. I'd like to share my story with you to encourage you to identify your dreams, seek them out, and achieve them, no matter what obstacles lie in your way, and remember, when He plants us and guides us through the harvest, the roast, and the grind, He's doing it for a reason.

CHAPTER ONE
REALIZING THE DREAM

After stepping off the train from my government job in Washington DC, I got inside my car, took a deep breath, and pulled out of the parking lot of the Metro to head home.

As soon as I arrived at the traffic light, as clear as day, I heard a voice speak to me.

"Open up a coffee house right over there."

I looked around. There was no one else in the car, no passenger beside me. Nobody outside. So I ignored the voice.

But then I heard the same voice speak to me again.

"I need you to open up a coffee house *right over there.*"

"There" happened to be an empty commercial space in my small town of Manassas, Virginia. Along with working in the federal government in DC, I was also a real estate professional, so I knew that it didn't make any sense to open up a coffee house, let alone *any* business, at that location; It had been vacant for over three years.

Still, I couldn't deny the conviction of that voice. It wasn't an audible one, rather, a voice within me that rose up and spoke from the inside out. This was the first time something like this had ever happened to me. Still, I knew I wasn't crazy.

I had to go home and tell my wife that something told me to open up a coffee house. But I was so surprised by what had happened, playing the voice over and over again in my mind, that I could barely drive the car. About a mile away from my home, I pulled off to the side of the road to get myself together before walking through the front door.

———

I remember when the seed of entrepreneurship was first planted in my heart: in Mrs. Thomas's third grade class, sometime after I returned from lunch and recess.

Out of nowhere, Mrs. Thomas had shouted, "Okay, class. I want everyone to say what you want to be when you grow up."

Many of the kids in class looked nervous, realizing they were about to be put on the spot. Me? I was terrified.

Susan was first. She looked at the teacher and stated boldly, "I want to be a nurse when I grow up."

Then the teacher called on Johnny.

With confidence, the next student named Johnny almost shouted, "When I grow up, I want to be a fireman!"

I remember locking eyes with the teacher. I knew for

sure I was going to be next.

"Okay, Kenneth, tell us what you want to be when you grow up."

My head and palms started to sweat. I froze for a second, and then I remember saying, "When I grow up, I want to be a businessman!"

Yes. I wanted to be a business…man!

———

Deep down in my spirit, I've always known that I didn't want to work for anyone, but because I'd never been exposed to any entrepreneurs, I did what people thought I should do to be successful. Years ago, I remember refreshing my resume and thinking to myself that my resume looked like the PA Turnpike Toll Ticket. This was primarily because I had been job hopping for years, going after money and opportunity, but I was never truly happy.

Then, when I was sixteen, I remember my girlfriend's grandmother telling us that she was going to take us to the big city of New York to see a play. I was excited because I had never been to New York. I also had never seen a play. I was in for a treat as well as a big life change.

You never forget the first time you see those huge buildings and people from all walks of life pressed together in New York City. The bus ride was only two hours long. "Wow," I kept saying to myself, "New York is so close to where I live, but I don't know much about this place."

I wasn't really sure exactly where we were going until the bus stopped and the bus driver yelled, "Welcome to the big city of New York! BROADWAY!"

I was sixteen and had never even heard of Broadway. And now, here I was, walking into a theater on Broadway. As we settled in our seats, I could feel the excitement in the air from the audience. I was still not sure what to expect before the lights dimmed and the curtain opened. My mouth dropped open in amazement.

Here I was, in New York City, seeing my first play, watching African American men and boys that looked like me and my family deliver such convincing, creative performances. I was totally drawn in and connected to the characters. The actor who played the father had a presence so powerful. His voice projected throughout the theater.

The whole time I kept thinking to myself, "I can do this!"

I wasn't sure why, though, because at that time I didn't sing, nor did I participate in school plays. But something happened inside of me once I saw that first play. When I finally looked at the playbill, I saw the title—*Fences*, starring James Earl Jones. It was an evening of firsts. It taught me that a life I couldn't imagine was out there, just out of reach, out of sight, and out of mind unless I put myself out there, committed myself to seeking it, finding it, exploring it, and thoroughly experiencing it.

Exposure in life and in business is valuable and necessary. Most of the time, when you get a vision, it's of things that you haven't experienced before. This normally brings about fear and will cause you not to believe and to run from your dreams rather than toward them. But, with just a little faith, you will see that the vision is really a roadmap to the things you need to get exposed to. Life is really an open book test. Just open your eyes and you will see the answers all around you. The question is, do you really believe?

FAST FORWARD

Two years later, I found myself peeking out of the hole of a snow-covered sleeping bag.

"Moorman! Moorman! Time for guard duty."

As I unzipped my sleeping bag, I experienced a type of cold like never before. It was more of a dry ice type of cold, one that pierces the bones.

I got dressed, put on my gear, and headed to guard duty. It was two o'clock in the morning.

I had joined the military after graduating from high school. Things hadn't gone as planned. I didn't get a basketball scholarship, and my parents couldn't afford to send me to college. I really didn't want to be a burden on them, so I made a hasty decision to join the army. I was eighteen years old and serving in Korea. Just two years prior, I had gone on my first trip to New York. New York was only two hours away from my house. Now, I was in another country. I experienced a huge culture shock, but the experience made me grow up fast.

I was assigned to a combat helicopter unit. I would hear them hovering over me all day. I used to write my cousin Sabu telling him, again and again, how much I wished I could be in college with him.

"What did I do to deserve this?" I remember asking myself over and over while in the field. I wasn't able to call home. I had no close friends or family. I was alone and lonely.

Immediately, I knew the military was not for me, but because of what my parents instilled in me, I knew I had to give my all to whatever I was doing. I had to stay and to do the best I could to succeed even though I wish I was almost any place but there. So I ended up actually excelling during my short time in the army. In fact they even wanted to send me to the leadership academy, but I knew I needed to be free. I knew I didn't want to work for anyone, but I was still wasn't sure what I was going to do with my life. I just knew whatever it was, it wouldn't involve the Army.

So, after leaving the military, I started to attend a junior college in Salina, Kansas. There, I majored in accounting with the hopes of getting a job in one of the big ten accounting firms one day. I was also the night auditor at the local bank. I ran the computer systems to update transactions and processed deposits. It was during this time that I discovered I had a singing gift.

I remember singing in the shower and in my room while in the military, but something happened one day. I realized I was able to imitate most singers. A friend heard me one day and was surprised. He asked me to sing a song while riding the bus to college in front of a large group of girls. I mustered up the courage to sing , and they couldn't believe what came out of my mouth. Neither could I!

A star was born!

Well, that's how I felt at the time. I knew I would have to pursue this newfound gift, so I started singing locally. Before I knew it, I was getting requests to sing everywhere. I sang at weddings, funerals, and on college campuses. I even sang in a traveling stage play.

Once I had seen that first play on Broadway, something was ignited inside of me, but soon after it had only smoldered. But now it was ready to burst into flames. All I had to do was see where my new-found talent would take me, and then to see just how far I could climb. I was about to be surprised.

DREAM REFLECTIONS

"Everything that happens in your life is supposed to happen. Those experiences are the lessons you need to learn to develop the skills and acquire the tools to accomplish your dreams and visions. Nothing that happens in your life is ever wasted!"

1. What did I take away from this chapter? What was the author's key message?

    _____

    _____

    _____

    _____

    _____

    _____

2. How does the author's story relate to my own personal story? Identify the seed that has been planted in you.

    _____

    _____

    _____

    _____

    _____

    _____

3. What action am I going to take to apply the information I just read?

_____

_____

_____

_____

_____

_____

COFFEE FACT

Merely smelling coffee can help wake you up.

Scientists have found that just inhaling a lungful of brewing coffee in the morning can activate your brain to better face the challenges and also opportunities of the day.

CHAPTER TWO
DREAM INTERRUPTED

In Spring of 1996, I moved to the city of big dreams and movie stars. Yes! I picked up and moved from Philadelphia to Hollywood, California to pursue a music career with my cousin Sabu and my high school friend ,Malik.

This was not the best time for me to be moving to another state. I had a two-year-old son, but I was still a young man trying to figure out how to make it for his family. My dad taught me to never sit around and watch things happen. All I knew was that a man was supposed to go and make things happen for his family. I was given this gift of singing; I knew I had to at least give it a try. Sabu, Malik, and I knew this was a long shot, but felt it was an opportunity we couldn't pass up. So I took a leap of faith and followed my dream.

I remember the moment I walked out of the LA airport for the first time. The sun was shining, and I experienced a different kind of energy, unlike anything I'd ever felt before. I couldn't take my eyes off of the beautiful palm trees and the amazing views as my cousin drove us around town. Even though there were a lot of unknowns, I felt I made the right decision moving to LA to pursue my dream.

To get by in LA, I worked in a clothing store on Melrose Ave, owned by our dear brother and friend, Kevin. Kevin had a heart of gold, and he really wanted us to run his shop so that he could spend more time with his wife and family. He played a huge role in my life. He was very successful in retail and poured all he knew and had into me. He showed me the ins and outs of how to run a retail business, but most importantly, he showed me how to run a business while loving others. He was my first exposure to the retail world, a world that I would soon get to know very well.

Along your journey there are people assigned to assist you and connect you to the next moment in your life.

After being in LA for a short while, we met two very talented guys, Christian and Idris. After deep thought and prayer, we asked them to join our group. Once they decided to join us in this part of our journey, we knew the group was complete. Our singing group name was Bottom Line. We were ready to take over LA.

When you add people to your vision/journey take time to meditate, pray or whatever you do to connect to yourself to make sure that you are connecting to right people. Most of the lessons learned as an entrepreneur will be connected to the wrong people you have in your circle. Choose wisely!

We put a plan together on how we were going to get a record deal. We gave ourselves two years to achieve this goal. We knew we could leverage Christian's connections in LA and his experience as a club promoter as well as all of the connects my cousin Sabu and Kevin made through the shop.

Working at the shop was a major opportunity for us. We would sing outside the shop doors on the sidewalk on Melrose Ave. Thousands of people walk Melrose Ave every day. This would bring in customers and also allow us to meet so many different people. Many were in the industry and would invite us to their events and private parties.

We wanted to be recognized as a group, so when we went out, it was always all five of us. We'd only go to the hottest clubs—and we *had* to have VIP access! Sometimes there would be forty or fifty people waiting in line to get into the clubs, but in we'd walk, past everyone, get to the front, and the bouncer would shake our hands, unlatch the rope, and just let us in. I could hear those in line saying, who are those guys? I guess you can say we had to fake it until we made it, but when it came to singing, we were ready! We looked great and also sounded great.

We worked out daily and rehearsed a lot to make sure we were ready whenever the opportunity would present itself.

When you have a dream you not only have to work on your craft or business, but you also must "get your hustle on." You have to put yourself in places where you can meet the people that can help you further your dream. You must leverage your contacts and relationships to help you look like you are already where you dream to be.

Well, needless to say, we did get a record deal, but after working on our album all summer in Atlanta, we received word that the record company wanted a crossover group and…decided to drop us from the label.

The guys in the group were devastated. We had sacrificed several years pursuing this dream. So I knew I was done with the music business for a while. I'd learned a lot. I wasn't sure how what I'd learned would serve me from here on out, but I learned something else—that I missed my son.

At this time my son was now five. I knew I could no longer *not* be in his life, so I moved back to the East Coast to be closer to my boy. In hindsight, the few years of hard work and dedication it took to get a record deal was easy. I quickly learned that keeping the deal is when the real work kicks in. The same is true in business. Most businesses fail within the first year.

Opening your business is not the final destination, it's part of the journey. Opening and sustaining a successful business is the goal you should be reaching for.

Now back in Philadelphia, I was trying to figure out what I was going to do. The one thing I was sure I could do is run a retail store.

I started applying for management positions. To my surprise, I was quickly hired with TJX Company as a store manager in one of their stores. Before I knew it, I was moving up the ladder quickly. I was the youngest General Store Manager in one of their new store divisions.

The principles that Kevin taught me while I was in California had come in handy. To succeed, all I needed to do was apply those principles, outwork everyone, and continue to love on people while doing so. I always applied these three principles: delegate, respect people, and always follow up! I couldn't believe I had 125 employees at one point. I was always accused of being "too nice," but for some reason, I still got results. I've always wondered who came up with this management rule that you have to be mean and disrespectful to get other humans to do something. I was determined to prove that theory wrong.

After several years of working for different retail companies, I knew it was time for a career change. I was good at retail, but I hated it with a passion. I had zero quality of life and missed all holidays and family events for years. I used to say I wanted to open my own store one day, but do it the right way.

On two different occasions I had customers approach me and suggest that I would be a good real estate agent. I will never forget the conversation I had with a real estate agent. I asked him why he became a real estate agent, and his response was this: "I want to be able to put my kids on the bus and be there when they get off."

That spoke volumes to me. I had never met anyone with that kind of flexibility and with an unlimited amount of earning potential. Suddenly, I knew that real estate would be my next move.

If you do more listening than talking, certain phrases,

words, and futures will stand out to you when people are speaking.

A few years went by, and my store was excelling in all areas (sales, employee retention, customer satisfaction, passing corporate audits). I started opening new stores for the company. Then, they would send me to other stores that weren't performing well. My store was also the district training store. Since I was young, I've always had the problem of getting bored once I've felt I have mastered a task or process. So the time came again when I felt I needed more from my job. Not to mention, I needed a higher salary!

I was tired of working in retail. I wanted to explore a new career. I remembered my conversation with the real estate agent and thought about following that path, but my work schedule was so busy, I never had time to take the two-week real estate course. It's a challenge to get out of retail. That left me feeling so frustrated.

Deep down in my spirit, I knew that one day I would make a living loving people.

Recruiters were calling me every day and I soon found myself accepting a store manager position for another retail company. I started this new company with a higher salary and less responsibility, but before I knew it, I was being relocated to Baltimore, Maryland to open up new stores for this company.

There are times in your life when you know a shift has taken place, and I definitely knew this decision to move to Baltimore was a shift. I wasn't sure what my future held, but I was expecting something great. My transition from Philadelphia to Baltimore was seamless. There was a freshness in the air in the suburbs where I lived. It was an excitement that I never felt in my life, and I was excited about starting a new job. I quickly dove into the job with all that I had. Young and fearless, I knew that I could outwork anyone at that time.

After hiring over one hundred employees, and a record-breaking grand opening, my career was on the highest level it could be in retail. But I didn't enjoy the business of retail.

I knew somehow, someway, I was going to make a living loving people.

I was working over seventy hours a week to maintain the excellence I had achieved. I was totally exhausted. I could feel my body starting to break down due to fatigue. Again, I was back on the cycle of missing every holiday for two years straight, being in the store, spending time with the employees and customers I loved, but I missed my family.

I was seeing my son, but not in the way or as often as I thought I would. In search of something more, I started to get back into singing. I even started recording music, and completed a project with some friends of mine who lived in Baltimore.

One of my employees would always come into my office and say, "Hey, Mr. Ken, I have someone I want you to meet." At this time, I was single, had been single for years, and everyone was trying to set me up. I didn't enjoy blind dates at all. They didn't seem to work for me, so I quickly declined. He came back the next month— this was a young man that I was mentoring—and he said, "Mr. Ken, I have someone in Manassas, Virginia that I *need* you to meet."

Again, quickly, I said, "Hey, man, I don't do hookups. Not for me."

The young man came back the next month, for the third time, knocked on my office door and said, "Mr. Ken, may I speak to you for a moment?"

"Sure," I said. "Come in." He looked me in the eye.

"Mr. Ken," he said, "I have your wife in Manassas, Virginia."

I looked at him. I asked him to shut the door and take a seat. After finding out what she looked like and getting additional details, I knew I had to meet this woman.

After exchanging numbers, Detra and I found ourselves talking for hours on the phone like teenage school kids. It was an exciting time for me because prior to that, all I did was work and make music. I quickly found myself traveling from Baltimore area to Manassas to visit her.

Our first date was at her church, which was a great experience. Then I found myself, for the first time in my life, going on coffee dates with her. Prior to that, I never really drank coffee. Even when we met, I think I ordered tea. I love to sing, so I'm always drinking tea. That was my earliest recollection of me meeting someone over coffee.

While our conversations continued over the course of the year, we grew closer. I knew this one was special. Detra was smart, driven, and most of all, I loved her heart. She had the gift of giving. Things continued to go well between the two of us, even though we lived in two different states.

I was still working over seventy hours a week at this point. Then, one morning, something happened. After doing a store set, working all night with my crew, I went home. When I woke up in the morning, I could not get up out of the bed.

Literally, I could not move. I had to call a friend to come help me get out of the bed. It was frightening. I considered myself to be in tiptop shape at the time.

My friend helped me to the hospital. After several doctor's visits, tests, and x-rays, I was diagnosed with a ruptured disc. I then found myself on disability, depressed, worried about how I was going to take care of myself, and deeply concerned as to what I was going to do next. But, I shifted my thinking as I had done time and time before. I told myself, *everything happens for a reason*, and suddenly, it became clear to me the reason for the ruptured disc. For the first time in years, I wasn't in retail! I had time to take the real estate test. Yes, the very test and industry that inspired me years ago. This, I figured, was my opportunity.

At the time, Detra was a heavy real estate investor. She and a group of women she worked with were very successful at buying and purchasing homes, selling them, and flipping them. It was amazing. She and I would talk about real estate all the time. She knew that I had always had a passion to become a real estate agent, so it was a no brainer.

"You'll get your license and I'll sell houses," she said. And that's what we did.

During my time on disability, I quickly took my real estate license, and passed it on the first try. And before you knew it, we were in business together. This was such an exciting time for us. The skies were the limit.

I would drive back and forth from Maryland to Virginia, twice a week, sometimes, to visit her and her son. Then I finally realized this was my opportunity to transition into a whole new career—a new life—that I loved.

I quickly rented a home in Manassas, temporarily, because I knew she was the one. After proposing to her within the year, we were quickly married in Jamaica in 2006 and on our way.

And wow, was life grand at that time! Real estate had taken off. It was at its highest peak price-point-wise in Northern Virginia. People were making money hand over. fist.

But no one could have ever anticipated what would soon happen. We had been in business for a year and had just purchased a new home, and then, before we knew it, we were in the middle of a financial housing crisis.

Things went downhill. Fast.

Other agents scrambled. My wife was trying her best to unload the inventory of homes that she owned. It was a tough time. We were newly married, had financial issues, were trying to stay positive, and also we discovered that our daughter, Kenadi, was on the way. Two years prior, it was just me. Now I had a family, and facing the biggest financial crisis I could ever imagine. We were over a million dollars in debt.

As a man, I wanted to fix this so badly, but I knew it was beyond me. I wasn't sure what to do.

During the housing crisis, things got so bad that I had to go back to the one thing I knew that I could do well: retail. In a flash, I found myself back to managing stores, working seven- plus hours a week, but this time, it was worse, as I had my own little family.

Deep down inside, I had enough faith to know that we would get through this. This was just a bump in the road, a season of faith-building, of truly believing in ourselves, and I knew there was still something inside I had to discover. I knew we had to go through this.

It was in the year 2009 that my wife asked me, "Have you ever thought about the federal government?"

Here I was, living in a government town, and it never once crossed my mind to apply for a job with the federal government. After thinking about it, I realized that by working in retail, I had developed so many transferable skillsets that could be valuable in the federal government. So I used all of my experience managing employees and my knowledge of human resources to apply for a job in the federal government.

I was quickly called in for an interview and was hired on the spot. And I worked just as hard, harder, even, than I always had. I had been in the government a few years doing HR Processing and various other tasks. My supervisor asked for a volunteer to run the help desk in the HR Department. My being ambitious, I quickly jumped on that, not knowing that it would eventually propel me to a new position in Program Management. I was soon managing HR IT systems in the federal government.

The thing is, I really didn't care for HR Processing or IT at all at that time. Deep in my spirit, I kept feeling the strong sense that this was not it. After being hired, I knew this was another shift in my life, another moment to recognize something special was happening. Still, deep down inside, I knew the federal government was not it, just a means to something greater. *Nothing's wasted.*

I kept getting promoted, kept getting higher grades, and money at that time in our life was not an issue. I mean, life was sweet. For the first time in my life, we weren't worried about bills. We recovered from the housing crisis, and my wife left her six-figure job to come home and homeschool the kids. Life was good. There was a big part of me that knew that we could just ride this out and live comfortably in the Northern Virginia area, but we both sensed there was something greater for us out there. Since it wasn't clear at that time, we continued with our day-to-day routine.

I started to notice on my daily train ride into Washington, DC the different people and their patterns. I could tell that they had no sense of their routine. They were locked into their lives. I suddenly felt like I was surrounded by a bunch of robots every day. Pleasant robots, robots that didn't respond, robots that slept every day on the train, totally exhausted, robots with very little expression. Even though I was the same train, I was determined to never become a robot.

DREAM REFLECTIONS

*Opening your business is not
the final destination, it's part of the journey.
Opening and sustaining a successful business is
the goal you should be reaching for.*

1. What did I take away from this chapter? What was the author's key message?

    _____

    _____

    _____

    _____

    _____

    _____

2. How does the author's story relate to my own personal story? Write out a list of your fears. There will be a transfer of power over them once you get them out of your head.

    _____

    _____

    _____

    _____

    _____

    _____

3. What action am I going to take to apply the information I just read?

_____

_____

_____

_____

_____

_____

COFFEE FACT

The word "coffee" comes from an Arabic word meaning "wine."

Some say the Arabic word *qahwah* means "wine," while still others insist it means "the wine of Islam." In the West for centuries, coffee was referred to as "Muslim wine." *Qahwah* became *kahve* in Turkish, which became *koffie* in Dutch and finally "coffee" in English

CHAPTER THREE
DREAM REVEALED

That was the day it happened: the day I heard the voice.

I knew I was not like the others. I was not destined to be a robot. The daily routine of the government was literally making me physically ill. Every day when I would sit down at my desk, I'd log into my computer and slowly feel the walls of that cubicle caving in on me, making it hard for me to think, making it hard for me to breathe. Some days I was actually nauseous at the overwhelming feeling of being caged. I desperately wanted to be free. But I wasn't sure how to achieve that freedom from such a secure place.

At this time, I'd been in the federal government for five years. I gained tons of experience in project management, and I developed a lot of new skillsets on top of everything else I had originally brought to the federal government. In the pit of my stomach, I still knew there was something else greater in me.

Once you receive that entrepreneurial bug it will never go away. You either starve it or feed it so it can grow.

The one thing I did while working for the government was maintain my real estate license through the housing crisis. Once the economy started to recover, we were on the cutting edge forefront, ready to start assisting customers and turn them into clients.

It was an exciting time, but very challenging. I was still in the government building, and realized there was very little cellphone reception in the area. Detra and I got creative! We had a routine. I would be standing on 14th and Constitution where there was cellphone reception, and I'd be making phone calls to clients, receiving them, booking appointments for real estate. We had the system down. As soon as I would get off the local train every day, my wife would have the list of appointments, and my route mapped out so I could quickly meet my clients. We were starting to build our real estate empire.

You see, I use the word "empire" because several years back, my wife and I were able to acquire over one hundred acres of land in Oxford, Mississippi, her hometown. Our true desire was to build neighborhoods, a mixed-use development where we could provide jobs for the local community there and give them opportunities. I tell you, there's something special about being able to stand on your land, look over the land, and envision it being built out in beautiful communities. This was an exciting time.

I couldn't believe that I actually owned land larger than the neighborhood that I grew up in.

I used to wish that my mom could see through my eyes and see what her baby boy had accomplished. This was amazing. Purchasing the land and then developing it was an incredible challenge. However, we both knew that it might not be for us to develop this land, but at least we had it available for our children.

The one thing that we all know is that they're not going to make any more land, so if you can buy a piece of land, grab it, hold onto it.

Real estate is all about timing. More and more people were starting to recognize us through real estate in Northern Virginia. It started to get challenging, juggling both full time federal government and real estate. I figured, this is it, this is what I must be doing. This is the little thing that's driving me crazy that I'm supposed to do. Real estate, yeah!

On this particular day, I was on the train ride home, totally disgusted about being in a place that I knew that I wasn't supposed to be.

Internally, I knew that I was supposed to make a move, but I wasn't sure what I was supposed to do. Glancing at all of the robots around me, I was determined not to be like that any longer. I call Washington, DC the city of blue, browns, and grays; when you look around, those are the major colors men that work for the government wear. I wore yellow shirts, just so that I wouldn't fit in.

That's when I got off the train, got into my car, took the deep breath, and pulled out of the parking lot of the Metro to go home. Then I heard:

Open up a coffee house right over there. I need you to open up a coffee house right over there.

None of it made sense. The timing was all wrong. But I knew it was something I needed to do.

Nervously, I pulled up to our driveway.

"Hey, Honey," I said. I remember, clear as day, greeting her with a big smile, her not knowing what I was getting ready to hit her with.

"What's up?" she said. "What's new?"

I asked her to sit down, and then I told her the story. She looked at me. I was nervous, because I knew that everything my wife was about to say would be right.

"This is crazy," she said.

I could see the fear in her eyes, the fear of the unknown. And then came an avalanche of questions. All her questions were valid, but I knew I could not ignore what I heard for the first time in my mind, in my heart.

"This is not the right time," she said. "What do you know about a coffeehouse? I just came home and left my six-figure job, to homeschool the kids. You're already doing real estate. Now this? Life is good. We're comfortable. We don't have to do anything else."

She was right on point. Our life was good, financially. We had money saved, no worries financially, and we were able to focus and be available for our kids. We didn't need to do anything for community or anyone else. But, again, I knew what I had heard and I was convinced.

"Okay," I remember telling her. "I won't do it. But you just remember, as we continue to pray to do all these different things, you remember that I came home one day and I told you that we're supposed to open up a coffeehouse. What would it hurt to just try and see? Make a few phone calls."

She looked at me with the strangest look. "Now is not the time."

"Okay," I said. "Just remember."

In my spirit, I knew that this would be something special, and to make it happen, I would need the support of my whole family—including the kids.

I got the point of my life where I didn't want to tell my kids to follow their dreams if they didn't see me follow mine. I had to be an example. I knew I had to lead the way for them.

While my wife was trying to figure out what just hit her, taking time to process the information I had just unloaded on her, I knew it was time for me to get busy.

Quietly, I started doing deep research on coffee houses. I had to totally immerse myself into the coffee culture. Thank God for Google and YouTube.

Once I started my search, I couldn't believe the amount of information there was about coffeehouses, about coffee beans, about coffee culture. Then I suddenly realized, through my reading and watching videos, that a whole language on coffee exists, one that I knew nothing about. I knew this was something serious. The one thing that I was confident about was the fact that I had succeeded in the past, and consequently, I could utilize my past experiences for my present venture. I knew that I could put together any retail store. I knew how to build teams, I knew the psychology behind it, and I knew profit and loss statements. Coupled with what I had learned in the government at that time about project management, your boy was well prepared. It didn't matter what I was selling. I knew how to build the right foundation to launch it.

When I closed my eyes, I could clearly see the vision. I could see the coffeehouse down to the colors.

When you get a vision, the vision is complete, but you can only see as much of the vision according to the amount of faith that you have at that time.

So, the more faithful I became, the more I believed, the more I could see the details come to life in my mind. I could see the colors of the chairs, as well as the type of chairs. I could see the flooring and the art. It was amazing, and I was excited.

During my research, I learned that there were so many coffee forums out there online: coffee chats. I quickly realized that coffee is part of every culture on earth. Different types of beans are grown in different places all over the world. I knew that coffee was the common denominator between all cultures, all races, and all religions. This was going be special.

I have seen tons of pictures online. I've watched so many videos. The one thing I noticed is I didn't see many African Americans at any of the coffee conferences or behind the bars as baristas. My only reference to coffee and an African American was Magic Johnson. I quickly realized, after learning the profit margin, why such a successful businessman put his money in coffee.

I started reading different stories about people who created coffee houses. There are few success stories. There are a lot of stories telling you why *not* to open a coffeehouse. Many people have had this dream, and failed for various reasons including but not limited to poor management of the inventory, poor employee relations, and, most of all, poor location.

I knew Jirani would have to be in the best location possible. Location was key. Similar to another familiar story, I started to realize that I wasn't getting into the coffee business—I was still in the real estate business. Location, location, location!

This goes back to my real estate background. The first thing we learn is one of the three golden rules of real estate. The first one is location, the second one is location, and the third is location. After getting over the shock of what I heard, I knew I needed to go and visit this place.

It just didn't make sense. It was a beautiful condominium building, five stories high with commercial units underneath. Every last one had been empty for the last two or three years. The business side of me just couldn't make sense as to why I would put a business here after no one else tried. This has been vacant for three years! Why me? Then, I heard a voice say, "Why not? Why not you? Who said you couldn't be the first, and succeed? Prove them all wrong."

Wow. I could hear new things now, which scared me. I had a new set of ears. This is the first sign of an important lesson that I learned about inspired businesses.

An inspired business will break every business rule at some point in time, and at different phases of your inspired business, you will be challenged with what you've learned in your past and taught in school to what your instincts are telling you to do. Inspired businesses force you to have an enormous amount of faith.

So, one might ask, what is an inspired business? To me, an inspired business is a business that came from the inside out. It's not something that you thought of, not something that you could say you created on your own, but something that you know, was given to you to do— too good for you to come up with on your own or invent. Yes, an inspired business is a precious gift.

I remember going to all of the units, and they were all empty. They didn't even have drywall yet. They were totally gutted out, brand new, never used for over three years. I started getting discouraged, but I still knew I had to at least try. You see, I can handle a "no," but what I can't do is deal with my not trying.

I found myself visiting those units often. I would walk around them many times, trying to get a feel of the traffic flow, how many cars would be part of this condominium unit, how many people actually lived in there. I remember talking to the manager, and I slightly hinted about what I wanted to do.

He almost begged me, "Will you please put a coffeehouse here? The residents would love it."

Oh, that was so exciting for me…to have my first bit of feedback be that my plan was on target. That there was a need.

A few months went by, and by this time, I had collected so much data on coffeehouses, furniture, equipment, and inventory needs, all the way down to the best type of napkins I should have. I remember watching a show on Oprah, and one thing she said stood out to me: "Love is in the details."

As a kid, when I would go to Disney World, I loved the rides. I loved the characters. It was just a fun time. But as an adult, when I take my kids, as the person who spends all the money, the thing that I appreciate the most are the details…from the Disney character–shaped bushes to the color of the straws, I love Disney World because of the details. Knowing this, I knew one of the things that would set my coffee house apart from the rest would be the details.

One day, out of the blue, I remember my wife asking me, "Hey, did you get any information about that coffeehouse thing?"

I looked at her in excitement.

"No, not yet," I said. "But I'm going to go ahead a make a few calls."

That, I knew, was my sign to go full steam ahead. Then I knew what was next. I needed to build a team.

DREAM REFLECTIONS

Once you receive that entrepreneurial bug it will never go away. You either starve it or feed it so it can grow.

1. **What did I take away from this chapter? What was the author's key message?**

    _____

    _____

    _____

    _____

    _____

    _____

2. **How does the author's story relate to my own personal story?**

    _____

    _____

    _____

    _____

    _____

    _____

3. **Define Believe. Spend time with the word**

Believe. Look up various definitions/ translations for Believe. Do I really believe in my dream?

_____

_____

_____

_____

_____

_____

4. What action am I going to take to apply the information I just read?

_____

_____

_____

_____

_____

_____

COFFEE FACT

Coffee has health benefits...

Coffee is packed with nutrients and antioxidants and has been linked with helping prevent diabetes, endometrial cancer, heart disease, liver disease, Parkinson's, and Alzheimer's. It also helps to burn fat.

CHAPTER FOUR
PAINTING THE DREAM

My daily Federal Government routine continued. I would get on the train with all of the other robots, including myself. Again, it's one thing to be a robot. It's another thing to *know* that you're a robot. That's the only way out.

During a training session, while rolling out this IT program for the Federal Government, one of my co-workers said to me, "Ken, where do you live?"

I told her where I lived at the time.

"Oh, wow," she said. "I live there, too."

"Oh, wow," I said. "That's amazing." She lived in the building where I was going to put the coffee house. So I got up the courage, and I whispered to her, "Hey, I'm thinking about putting a coffeehouse in one of the units where you live."

Oh, how her eyes lit up with excitement. She couldn't believe what I had said.

She said, "Ken, that's amazing. You can do it. If you can, do me a favor. I need you to come to a meeting tonight."

"What kind of meeting?" I said.

"Well, I'm also on the school board for the City."

I said, "Oh, I didn't know that."

"Yes," she said. "We're having a meeting. I want you to come."

I couldn't figure out why would I show up at this meeting. My kids were homeschooled. It just didn't make sense. I'm a guy that wants to keep his word, so I said, "Okay, maybe after work."

She said, "Ken, you have to show up. You need to show."

I said, "Okay."

I got off the train that evening and I thought the meeting was at the high school. So I went to the high school. Nobody was there. At this time, it was 7:30 at night. I'd been on the train since 5:30 in the morning. It had been a long day. I headed home. But while I was driving home, something told me, "Go to City Hall." When I went to City Hall, to my amazement, I saw my co-worker and a few other people in the vestibule, talking.

I parked the car. As I started walking up, we connected eyes and she waved me into the vestibule. When I walked in, she said, "Hey, Ken. Hey, everybody, I want to introduce you to Ken. Ken, this is the school board," and she says, "Everyone, Ken is going to be opening up a coffee house right over there."

Inside, I was terrified. I didn't want everyone to know because even though I knew I *had* to do it, I wasn't sure if I was going to! But now the cat was out the bag.

To my surprise, they were so excited. They were like, "Great. We need it. We have to do it." I couldn't believe the response.

Then she told me, "Ken, go inside. They're in session. Go in there and have a seat." I was like, "Okay," still not knowing why I was at this City meeting. I went into the session. I saw the Mayor, the City Council, and I saw someone presenting something to the Council about some needs and some things they wanted to get done in the city.

The whole time, I was trying to figure out why she told me to come here.

I was sitting there while they were talking about some real estate stuff and I thought, oh, I probably need to know this for the land that I want to develop in Mississippi. I sat for a little while longer. Then my friend came in and waved me outside to meet someone. I got in the hallway, and she said, "Ken, this is John."

I said, "Oh, how you John?"

"John," she said. "Ken is going to open up a coffee house right over there at City Center. John looked at me in excitement.

He said, "Ken, do me a favor. All I need you to do is try."

"Okay," I said.

"Seriously," John said, "All I need you to do is try. Just do me that favor."

I said, "Okay. Sounds good. All right."

When John walked way, I asked my friend, "Who was that?"

She said, "Oh, that's the City Lawyer."

I said, "Oh, okay. Wow."

And then another woman walked up. My friend flagged her over ,and she said, "Hey, Darlene, I need you to meet Ken Moorman." Then she told Darlene, "Darlene, guess what? Ken is going to open up a coffee house right over there at City Center."

Oh, my eyes got big. I was like, she's telling *everybody*. I don't want anyone to know yet. I'm not sure. Darlene looked at me in excitement.

And she, too, said, "Ken, please just do me a favor. Just try. Ken, do me that favor. Just try. Whatever resources you need, just let me know. Ken, I am the City Manager. Whatever resources you need, let me know."

I said, "Okay. Great." She looked me in the eye and said just what John had said.

"Do me a favor. Just try."

By the time I walked out of City Hall, I was convinced that I was going to open up a coffee house.

Being in the right place at the right time is an understatement for entrepreneurs. It's everything! Most entrepreneurs are alone with our dreams but to take it to the next level you must be prepared and show up!

It had been over a year since I had heard the voice. After my experience at City Hall, I knew it was time to build a team. One thing I know is that if you have a vision or a dream, you must know that it takes a team in order to help you get the dream off. If your dream is big enough for you to carry, it's not big enough. Dream bigger.

After church one day, we finished worship, and I was talking with my dear friend, my brother, the worship pastor, and I knew he had a love for coffee that I've never seen before. He lived in Seattle, he knew all about the coffee culture, everyone knew him. Everyone knew that he was the coffee guy.

We were talking, and I slightly hinted to him that, hey, I've been working on something for a year, brother, and I'm going to open up a coffee house.

His eyes lit up. He got so excited. He started to tell me that, "Man, I've been dreaming of doing this. But I don't know much about business."

I said, "Hey, I don't know anything about coffee. But I do know business. Let's do this together."

Oh, we started to talk it through, and just think about the different things we could do with music to pull in the community. It was a great thing. He was all in. He immediately started to send me all different types of information on coffee: origin, how it's made, lattes, drip coffee…it was amazing. I was excited. I was more convinced that I knew I had the tools to make this happen.

After a few months went by, we had a serious talk, and he hinted to me that he felt that he was being led to move back to Seattle with his family. He was so torn because this was a dream of his to be a part of a community coffee house. But deep inside, he knew it was time for him to move his family back to Seattle. I was so happy for him because I knew the desires of his heart, and I never get in front or in the way of someone else's vision.

Quietly, I was deeply disappointed. I was scared. Fear started to kick in. How in the world am I going to do this alone? I don't know anything about coffee. What am I going to do without him? Every time I thought about quitting, I wouldn't be able to sleep. But at this point, I was so far in, I knew I could not stop. So, I continued to build my team.

DREAM REFLECTIONS

Along your journey, there will be people that will be assigned to you to help support you just for a season in different parts of your journey. The sooner you learn to let them go, the better. Hold on to no one and enjoy and love on them much as you can, while they're in your presence.

1. What did I take away from this chapter? What was the author's key message?

   _____

   _____

   _____

2. How does the author's story relate to my own personal story?

   _____

   _____

   _____

3. List the first seven things that come to mind about your vision/dream. What do you see when you close your eyes?

   _____

   _____

   _____

4. What action am I going to take to apply the information I just read?

_____

_____

_____

COFFEE FACT

The "Americano" came about because American soldiers in WWII found espresso too strong.

Not used to the fulsome sting of full-blooded espresso, American GI Joes during World War II used to request it be watered down significantly—thus the "Americano" was born. It's also the origin of the term "cup of Joe."

CHAPTER FIVE
THE DREAM TEAM

While I was dealing with my disappointment and excitement, a sister friend of ours went back to school and completed her degree in interior design. She was super talented, but being a little older than the average college graduate, she was finding it difficult to find jobs in that field. She was passionate about interior design. She was the first person that I contacted. I was so nervous to tell her about the vision I received about this coffee house because she was very close to us, and she knew that we had never talked about a coffee house. I didn't want it to seem crazy, or some get rich quick thing.

In my spirit something told me, "just share the story." Just tell the story. So, that's what I did. I met with her, I shared the story and the vision, and immediately she was grateful for the opportunity. That's when I knew that this coffee house was going to be for entrepreneurs and other small businesses to work together to achieve something great. I quickly learned that it's easier for entrepreneurs to ride the wave together and share resources instead of one person trying to do it all. I knew I would need a general contractor that would work with me, and one that I knew I could trust.

I started to get several bids from different

recommendations, and I ran across a dear friend of mine from church. Many people gave him great references and I knew he would be the one. I shared the story with him as well. Immediately, he was super excited and on board.

Picking the right team that really buys into and supports your vision, and doesn't attempt to steer it one way or the other, is critical to the success of your business. Especially in the initial phase.

Things started to take off fast. Once you start putting legs under your vision, be ready.

I remember my wife telling me, "You need help. You can't do all this alone while still working real estate. You need some help."

But deep down inside, I really didn't want any help, because this was my thing. It was going to sustain me and bring income in, and I didn't want to split the money. It wasn't about money, but I couldn't see how I was going to make it if I had to share any of the profits.

I was giving Dwayne, the one who moved to Seattle, an update of what had been going on.

He said, "Hey, I think you need to meet Jesse. He's a good guy, and he's looking to do something in the coffee field as well. You need to check out Jesse."

Time went by, I got busy, started bringing on different team members, and I forgot about calling Jesse. Dwayne asked me again about a month later, "Hey, did you reach out to Jesse?" I said, "Oh, I'm going to do it today."

After meeting Jesse, I immediately knew there was something special about him. Like everyone else, all I did was share the story. He immediately gravitated to it. He was willing to help in any way. He didn't want anything in return—he really just wanted to be a part of something special.

We walked around the building several times, looking at the site, and he was excited. I could tell that he was a man of honor. He was a Naval Academy graduate, wore his heart on his sleeve, and had a passion for people in his own special way. For this vision, I truly needed someone that I could trust, and that would get behind the vision and support in any way. I knew he was the one.

After some time of praying about it on both sides, I asked him to come on and take a bigger role to help me roll out this vision. Not to mention, I quickly realized that he was a quiet genius. He was very detailed and had an eye for quality in all things.

Everything in excellence was the one thing I said after every meeting until we opened.

Through recommendations and talking to different people, the team began to grow quickly; store manager, shift managers, architect, and a marketing manager. I knew that branding would be the key to the initial phase of this project. When people walked into the coffee shop I wanted them to feel like there were two thousand of them already. *Everything in excellence. Nothing less.*

Once the team was formalized, we met in my house

once a month for eight months, talking about every detail of the coffee shop. We started with ourselves because we were all customers. We asked ourselves what we liked and disliked about coffee houses. What would we want in our coffee house? More importantly, what did our community need in the coffee house? It was amazing to me how excited they all were about the vision. And they all were super talented in their fields, too.

I felt blessed. The word started to get out that there was something special on the way, and many people were telling me, "Hey, I would love to help you. I don't do this. I don't do that. But let me know if there's something I *can* do." I remember going to my church one early Sunday morning and seeing a group of women praying over the seats of the empty chairs before the people started arriving.

I asked someone, "What are they doing?" I was quickly told about the prayer team and how they prayed for everyone before they came there. I was also informed that they took prayer requests.

That just blew me away. I couldn't believe there were people assigned to just pray for people they don't even know, all the time, every day. All of a sudden, something clicked. I knew that would be my secret weapon, that would be my covering, to have the prayer team, a group of people that believe in the vision, but their gifting was prayer. Through meeting certain people and different relationships I had with many prayer warriors, I asked them if they would be part of the coffee house prayer team. They were so excited. We didn't have to meet. All we did was create a group on text, and I would text prayer requests to them for the needs of the coffee house. This was the most powerful aspect of the team.

When you have an inspired business, you have to quickly learn how to push through obstacles, especially in the beginning. If you find yourself redirecting your vision, stopping, not moving forward, you will continually receive obstacles. You have to remember that your business is inspired, so there is a force out there that would love for you not to do what you feel you were called to do. Push through any and all obstacles!

The time had come when we needed to get inside of the space. The architect needed access to the space to do measurements and to get a better feel of what would be needed. For some reason, the realtor would not meet us. Every time we set a schedule, he wouldn't show. Then once we finally got inside of the space that we wanted, he kept trying to suggest that we take the smaller one on the other side.

We shared the vision, we told him we would need a little more space to do community events.

He said, "I think you guys should take the smaller one."

You have to really stay firm on your vision. People will try to divert it or make it make sense for them. This just wasn't working. I couldn't understand why he wouldn't want to give me the space since I was the only business applying. I needed additional information to move forward from the realtor.

After going back and forth, the team agreed we would look at other places. After thinking about different locations, we went into Old Town Manassas. I actually lived fifteen minutes from Old Town Manassas, but I never really came down here for any events. To my surprise, this place was beautiful. I knew that this would be a perfect spot for a coffee house.

We found a place that was available for rent. It would need a total rehab, and the cost would be enormous. The great thing, though, was that it was right next to the pavilion. It was going to be two levels with windows on the side to overlook the pavilion. We were excited. But for some reason, we could not get the owner to see the vision. She did not want us to put a coffee house there. (In hindsight, it was a blessing because that would have been a nightmare.)

So, we went to the next building on the corner across from the pavilion, a beautiful building, two stories. I remember the owner saying, "Hey, I don't want you to tear my building up." But he believed in the vision and offered any resources that he had. I knew this was special because I started to see people in business do stuff that wasn't normal. They wanted to support us even if there was no financial gain in it for them.

Frustration started to set in because I knew this was something we were supposed to do, and I knew this was the place for the site of the coffee house. One early morning I was walking in Old Town, just trying to get a sense of traffic and the community, and I walked past the building right at the train station. To my surprise, it was available. I couldn't believe it. I got excited. Being in real estate, I quickly looked it up online and I saw the additional details. This could be the space.

I made a call. The space was available immediately. I knew we had to get this space. Once the realtor let us inside of the unit, and we walked around. We knew it would need a lot of rehab, but this was the perfect size and the perfect location.

The only thing: it was six months sooner than when we were ready. But we knew this unit would not last, so we jumped on it. We got the lease six months prior to us being ready to start the build out. But we had to factor that into our build out plan. We had to hold on to this unit because this would be the future site of the number one coffee house in Northern Virginia.

I still remember the first time I walked into the shop after signing the lease. This used to be a boutique, so it had a lot of different small rooms you could walk in and out of, but I still could see what this coffee house would look like. I knew we were going to have to tear down everything in there, all the walls, and start from scratch. I was up for the challenge. We had just signed the lease, and I was ready.

———

Time passed. A couple months went by. I was now ready to start setting dates for the team as to when we were going to start the build out, when we would start hiring the crew, even down to ordering supplies. I mean, I had it all laid out. One thing you have to know, if you don't set a date, you'll never reach it. So I was okay with setting a date to push the team. The whole team kept saying this was unrealistic, but I knew that I controlled the date. We would get more done by that date, and I could just push the date back if needed. With that said, I might have pushed that date back three times or so, but it was for good cause.

For whatever reason, I had done many build outs before to schedule and to plan. But this time, everything took a little longer. Why? I knew this wasn't on my timing. That's how I also, without a question, knew this was an inspired business. We would do our due diligence, press toward our schedule, if things didn't work out according to plan, we would just readjust and go from there. As things started to progress, I realized that I really didn't have time to do real estate, to also complete this build out and, simultaneously, continue to work in the government. But more than anything, in my spirit, I knew I had to be present during this build out. I had to make sure my heart was in this one.

When you're the visionary, and you have a great team behind you, walking alongside of you, you almost get the sense they're truly counting on you to complete what everyone has started. That is the moment you feel deep in your spirit that you have to complete your dream because others dreams are tied to your dream. It's not even about you anymore!

When things got rough and I would be down on

myself, I could see the team members. I could see their smiles, I could see and hear their voices, and even feel their belief and commitment to this project. I would all of the team's passion around opening this coffee house and then use that to motivate me to stay up later at night, to be more detailed, to follow through with the things they asked me to do.

I was blessed. I had the best team.

"May your good be better and your better be blest." –Eddie Murphy in "Holy Man."

DREAM REFLECTIONS

1. What did I take away from this chapter? What was the author's key message?

    _____

    _____

    _____

2. How does the author's story relate to my own personal story?

    _____

    _____

    _____

3. If you can carry a dream by yourself then your dream is too small. List who you want to be on your team.

    _____

    _____

    _____

4. What action am I going to take to apply the

information I just read?

_____

_____

_____

COFFEE FACT

Only two U.S. states grow coffee.

Kona coffee is the United States' gift to the coffee world. Because coffee traditionally grows best in climates along the equator, Hawaii's weather is optimal for harvesting coffee beans. Recently, California also got into the coffee game with dozens of farms now churning out pricey bags of the stuff.

CHAPTER SIX
ALL IN ON THE DREAM

The time had come for me to start planning on making the jump. Yes, it was time to leave the federal government. I had been planning for this moment for over a year. The date was set: October 2, 2015 was going to be my last day in the federal government.

If you don't set a date for the things you want to accomplish they will never get done!

I had a few months left, and I started to experience sleeplessness. When I did fall asleep, I would wake up in a sweat. It was like I knew I was getting ready to jump off a cliff without a parachute. No guarantees, nothing but a dream, a whole lot of preparation, an awesome team that believed in the vision, and the support of my family. When you get the support of your family, you can do anything.

I had my logo complete. A year prior, I had the logo of the coffeehouse on my cell phone as the wallpaper. I looked at this logo every day for one year. I could feel I was getting closer. I secured the building. I was getting ready to transition from the federal government to full-time entrepreneurship, and I couldn't believe it. The closer I got, the more I believed. It was amazing. I remember finally breaking down and telling my manager my vision and my dream for a coffeehouse. To my surprise, she was in full agreement.

> *It's one thing to write down your vision and your plan, but something special happens once you start speaking out your vision.*

Now more things began to align. People start to react in ways that they're not used to reacting toward your vision. These people are inspired. Your conviction becomes their commitment and even participation in your dream. This is about you ready to share your dream with confidence, clarity, and unstoppable commitment.

You literally have to speak out your vision for it to become a reality. If it's stuck in your head, it will stay in your head. If you take a deep look and self-assess your life, you will realize that throughout your lifetime everything that you have accomplished is a direct reflection of what has or hasn't come through your heart and then out of your mouth. Words are powerful! Once you fully understand and accept that spiritual principle you will quickly start to be more intentional about the words that you allow to come out of your mouth. Do *everything* with intent!

After a month or so, my manager called me into her office. She motioned me when I arrived to shut the door, and then looked me in the eye and said, "You have to jump."

I responded, "What do you mean?"

She repeated, "You have to jump. You have to follow your vision. This is not the place for you. The community needs you."

I could not believe it. I was so concerned about leaving my job. I knew that my manager had many spiritual gifts so I just had to trust her with my dream. I was in awe. But this was just another sign to let me know that I was on track, that my vision was on point, and this was something that I *must* do... now.

————

A few weeks later I awoke one morning just staring at the alarm clock, looking at the time. The alarm clock went off and I immediately hit it. It stopped. I looked at my cell phone and realized *today was the day*: October 2, 2015, the day I was going to jump. Today was my last day at the federal government. I woke up numb, just not feeling myself. An array of emotions were going through my body. Happiness, fear, anxiety, thinking I was crazy – all of these emotions were colliding together. But I knew it was something I had to do. Then excitement came over me and, finally, a sense of peace overwhelmed me.

I got dressed. It was raining outside, but I didn't care. I was going in to wrap things up. My last day at work was surreal. People were looking at me with deep admiration. They were proud of me that I had the courage to step out. Some, I knew I would be friends with for life. At the end of this last day at work, I remember walking outside, the rain splashing down in my face -- something told me to capture this special moment.

————

Years ago, when I was in the music and entertainment world, my life went by so fast. I didn't really capture much of that time. So I promised myself, going forward I was going to capture the special moments in my life. I vowed to burn my important milestones deep into my heart.

When you are really present and living in the moment, you can tell when you are transitioning from one phase of your life into another.

I knew this phase would change my life forever. I also knew on the other side of me walking out of this door was a new Ken. I gave myself a new beginning. I would capture the moment, so I grabbed my cell phone and I started recording how was feeling. I wanted to thank all the people who had helped me get this far, who had supported my vision, and also my family and the community. It was amazing. I captured it and saved it for myself.

Just before I got on the train ride home, I texted the video to my wife just so she could see it. Once she saw it, she immediately texted back... *post it.*

I hesitated. *I'm so nervous,* I texted her back. *I didn't do this for the world. I did it for me.*

Post it. It will bless people.

I really didn't understand it. It took me a while. In fact, it took me the whole train ride home. But I got up the courage and I posted it.

My inbox flooded. So did my timeline. People were shared how my message had brought them encouragement. They could not believe that I had the courage to do something so grand, to leave the federal government, to follow my dream and passion. Again, another sign that I was aligned with my vision and this was something that I must do.

I remember waking up to my alarm clock the morning *after* I made the big jump from the federal government. I started getting myself ready to go to work and quickly realized I was free. I didn't have to do that anymore. It was a feeling that's very hard to explain, knowing that I was in total control of my destiny, walking in my purpose. I was confident. I was fearless. I knew this was the right time in my life to do what I was supposed to do. The next phase was the build out. I had the team put together. Equipment was arriving at the shop, and the main key was that I knew I had to be present in all phases of this build out.

DREAM REFLECTIONS

Do EVERYTHING with intent!

1. What did I take away from this chapter? What
    was the author's key message?

    _____

    _____

    _____

2. How does the author's story relate to my own
    personal story?

    _____

    _____

    _____

3. Conduct a self-assessment of the words that
    are coming out of your mouth. Are you
    speaking positive words that can bring life to
    your dreams or are words of doubt and fear
    being spoken into the universe?

    _____

    _____

    _____

4. **What action am I going to take to apply the information I just read?**

_____

_____

_____

COFFEE FACTS

Decaf does not mean caffeine-free.

An eight-ounce brewed cup of decaf coffee actually contains two to 12 milligrams of caffeine. In comparison, a regular cup of coffee supplies between 95 to 200 milligrams, while one can of cola only has 23 to 35 milligrams of caffeine.

CHAPTER SEVEN
NIGHTMARES

About a week after leaving the federal government, I got a call from my sister saying that my mom was having a procedure, and she thought my brother and I should be there to support her. You see, my mom was diagnosed with pre-onset Alzheimer's at the early age of sixty. She was now sixty-nine.

I remember telling my wife and kids, "Hey, I'm going to see Nana, I'll just be there for the procedure on Friday."

Then my sister called on Friday before I had time to go see mom. She said, "Hey, I think you guys really need to get here to make sure everything's okay." So I jumped in the car immediately.

On my way there, I started to reminisce all of the great talks my mom and I had throughout the years. I remembered how she always made me feel like I was the best thing. She encouraged me. My father taught me how to be a provider, but my mom taught me how to love. I couldn't understand why this trip was so emotional for me. I chalked it up to all of the transition I was going through with leaving the job and thinking about all of the unknowns. I had all these people following me and believing in me and the cause, so I figured that was why there were so many emotions.

Anyway, I get to the hospital where I sat in the parking lot for awhile. I wasn't ready to go in because I really don't like hospitals. I wasn't ready to see my mom there, but I knew it was something I had to do. I went inside to the front desk and gave them my mother's name to find out what room she was in. Then I went upstairs, got off the elevator and I started looking for her room. I walked slowly past each room, 234, 236, 238. I got to what I thought should have been my mother's room but I wasn't sure, I looked to my right and there was a nurse's station. Directly in front of me I could see a room that was open.

I could see feet, then the curtain was pulled and I could see feet beneath the curtain, moving around, kind of rapidly. Right outside the door I could see someone that appeared to be a clergy member, a priest, in all black with a collar, white collar.

I walked up to the priest and said, "Is this Joyce Moorman's room?"

He looked at me. I looked around. My brother and sister weren't there. It was just me and the priest in front of this room.

He nervously said, "Excuse me, who are you?"

I said, "Well, I'm her son. I came from Virginia to be here for her procedure." I could see his hand start shaking as if he was getting nervous.

I looked underneath the curtain. I could see the feet

moving rapidly like they were wrapping up something, like something was finished in there, and they were cleaning. I wasn't sure, but all of this was going on at the same time that thoughts were in my mind trying to figure out, *why is the priest looking at me like this? Why is he here? What are they doing in that room if this is my mother's room?*

The priest looked at me with the sincerest look you can give someone and said, "I'm sorry, Mr. Moorman. Your mom just passed."

My heart dropped. I wasn't sure how to process what he just told me.

I looked for my brother and sister. Why am I the only one here? Why did I have to be the first one to receive this news? I was devastated. Then it dawned on me that as I was walking up they had just unplugged the respirator and my mom just passed.

So many thoughts went through my mind. *Why didn't I come up sooner? Why did I delay? Why am I here alone? Why did she just wait for me before she crossed over?* I couldn't believe it. I then realized what lay ahead. I had to turn around and tell my sister and brother that mom had passed. I didn't know what to do.

I walked aimlessly back down the hallway and about fifty feet away my sister and brother in law exited off of the elevator. We locked eyes and I didn't know what to say. My sister knew it. She fell down and collapsed.

She said, "She's gone."

My sister and my mother were so close.

I was heartbroken because I knew my sister not only lost her mother, she just lost her best friend. At that moment I knew being the youngest sibling, I would have to be strong for my sister and my brother and my family. I had to gather myself because I knew my brother was on the way.

Before I knew it, he got off the elevator and I was standing right there. He had no idea what I was getting ready to tell him. I remember it like it was yesterday.

"What's up, bro?"

He looked at me, and all I could say was, "Bro, she's gone." I could see him trying to reason what I was talking about. I said, "Bro, she's gone. Mom's gone."

He broke down. At six feet four, two hundred plus pounds, he fell into my arms. It was a moment that I'll never forget. I knew I had to be strong for my family.

After celebrating my mom's crossover into eternity, I really just wanted to take some space, but I wasn't sure where to go or what to do. I had left the government two weeks prior to start an adventure that was new. Now my life was totally new with the absence of my mother, and I was trying to figure all this out. It was such a trying time but the one thing that I couldn't deny despite all of the tragic emotions I was feeling during the grief, was that my vision was still there. The coffeehouse still had to be built and there was no one else to do it but myself. I knew I had to be the one to drive this vision to fruition.

When you get a vision and the moment you truly in your heart accept that vision, it doesn't matter what's going on in your life, that vision will become a thorn in your side until it is birthed. It will either go to someone else or you're going die with that vision inside of you.

So, without even thinking twice, I quickly came back, got inside of the space, and immediately started to birth Jirani Coffeehouse.

DREAM REFLECTIONS

When you get a vision and the moment you truly in your heart accept that vision, it doesn't matter what's going on in your life, that vision will become a thorn in your side until it is birthed. It will either be given to someone else or you're going die with that vision inside of you. You Choose!

1.   What did I take away from this chapter? What was the author's key message?

_____

_____

_____

_____

2.   How does the author's story relate to my own personal story?

_____

_____

_____

_____

3. Identify the thorn in your side. What is the one thought/vision/dream that won't go away no matter what is happening in my life?

    _____

    _____

    _____

    _____

4. What action am I going to take to apply the information I just read?

    _____

    _____

    _____

    _____

COFFEE FACT

Dark roast is weaker than light roast.

When it comes to coffee, the darker the berry, the weaker the juice. Stick to the light blends if you want a caffeine jolt that will rattle your tooth fillings loose.

CHAPTER EIGHT
LUCID DREAMS

I was working day and night with my team that was right with me. Everyone was doing what they were called to do, *in excellence*. That was our motto. I started every meeting with the words "Everything in excellence" and I ended every meeting saying, "Everything in excellence." Most of the time when you receive a vision it's sent to you and you only, and as you start to walk out your vision, if you're connected to it, you'll soon see that people will come into your life to add to your vision. People with skillsets that you could never obtain are all of a sudden willing to lend their skills to your vision. That's when you know you're on the right track.

One thing I quickly learned was that just because I could do it, it didn't mean that it was for me to do. You start to realize that your vision and dream are tied to other people's visions and dreams. I knew the build out initially wouldn't be a challenge for me because I had done it for years for TJX companies—building out new store sets, hiring, and dealing with contractors. My team would have a building of 100,000 square feet and build it out within two months with no problem, so I felt prepared. I was equipped.

I would always put dates before the team because

again, if you don't put a date on something, you'll never reach it. However, as a month went by and then two months I noticed that we weren't making the type of progress according to the project plan or the timeline that I had set, so I did what I was trained to do. I doubled the force; talked to the general contractor and he got more people in there to make up on time. Time was ticking. At this time we were paying a monthly lease, so we had to wrap this thing up.

No matter how many people we put on an assignment, for some reason it would still move at the same pace. Then I realized that I was forcing it. I wasn't going with the natural flow of this inspired business. We took a step back and decided we were going to take our time and cover every detail. We knew that this place would be special. We started the build out and the community started to get curious. I could see them with their face pressed against the glass trying to look in to see what this was going to be. Something in my spirit said, "Let them in." I would welcome and greet the customers and they would quickly ask, "What is this?" I would explain, "It's Jirani. It's a coffeehouse. It's your coffeehouse."

I started to give tours of the coffeehouse before the items were there. I would walk them to the left side and say, "There's going to be a fireplace here. There's going to be a soundstage over here. This is going to be a meeting space." I could see in their eyes that they were trying to picture what it would be like, even though they were only looking at bricks and no walls at the time. I started to notice people would come back at least once a week to see the progress. Once the fireplace went up, they were like, "The fireplace is here! Oh wow, this is the stage! I see the framing." They really got excited once they saw the bar, the coffee bar. That made it all true to them. There was really going to be a coffeehouse in their neighborhood.

I remember starting to put the bricks up the wall. By this time the community kept saying, "Please let us be a part of this. This is going to be special." And I didn't know what I could do. Then I had a great idea. "Hey, we'll let you guys come in and put the bricks on the wall." We now have this large area of brick inside the building on the left side where two-thirds of it was put up by the community. They brought their kids in to the nook area where the bricks were and together, families would put in the bricks. It became a family thing to pour into something in their community.

The equipment we ordered started to pour in. I remember the big box came in with the espresso machine, and "the heart of Jirani" on the coffee side. As the furniture and chairs arrived, I just couldn't believe I was touching what I was seeing in my vision. There aren't many words to truly describe that feeling, but I knew we were going to get this done.

I spent a lot of time in the shop alone building it out, and the grief would come down on me pretty heavy sometimes, so I just poured it into the walls of that place. I would talk to my mother as I was putting bricks on the wall. I would talk to my mother as I was sweeping the floors, and say, "I'm doing this for you." I always wanted my mom to be proud of me. She did so much for me. I wanted to show her that I was going to complete this in her name.

Time was going by. The build out was going well. I would come into the shop some mornings or some afternoons and I would see contractors or different team members giving the community the same tour they saw me giving people every day. It was contagious. People were fully invested in this vision. They were sharing the vision with the community, and I wasn't there.

"When you have a vision all you have to do is tell the story. Don't sell it. Just tell it."

Well, the build out took five months and the place was gorgeous. It was the best coffeehouse any of us had ever seen. The community could not believe what was coming for them. They were ready. There was a time when the city would have a big festival outside and we didn't even have walls. I set up tables outside of the shop and I had employees and team members go out and we literally handed out 5,000 punch cards. I told the team it was important that you don't just set the cards down on a table. I need you to hand it, look at someone in the eye, and tell the story of Jirani.

By the time we had our grand opening, the place was full. Over 200 people showed up to the grand opening. The mayor, senators, and local media all came. It was a big deal and in my eyes I looked around holding back my tears. During this grand opening I had so many words to say and so many things to share and so many people to thank. The team that I had was so incredible. I'm forever grateful for them. As I was saying my thank you speech to everyone that came to the grand opening, I realized that people were hanging onto my every word. They knew and could see someone that went at their dream and had obtained it. At the moment I knew there was a transfer of power unto myself to do the next biggest thing. As I closed my speech, I ended it with these words, "Thank you for sitting in my dream."

During the build out process, different people in the community would come through and give me all types of words of encouragement to continue on doing what I was doing. One day this one man in the community really blessed me, which made me realize this was going to be something special. I was actually in the shop alone, up on the ladder putting up the last few bricks on the wall, my face covered in dust. I went outside to get a breath of fresh air. When I looked to the right, I saw an older African American gentleman looking at the historical information stand that gave historical facts about the train station.

Manassas, Virginia, has a rich Civil War history, but there's another part of the story that isn't always told. This older gentleman, he looked to be about 80 years old, looked well kept, looked at me and then walked over to me slightly bent over and he said, "What is this young man?"

I said, "Excuse me sir?"

"What is this?"

"Sir," I said, "this is going to be a coffee house."

"A coffee house?"

"Yes, sir, it's going to be a coffee house for the community where everyone comes and they can relax, enjoy the arts, and it's a place for people to come together."

He looked at me. He looked deeply into my eyes and he said, "Do you know what you got?"

I said, "Excuse me sir?"

He said, "Do you know what you got?"

I said, "Uh sir, a coffee house? I'm not sure."

He said, "No." He said, "Do you know slaves were sold right there?"

He was pointing over at the Manassas train station (approx. 20 feet away), and I immediately got the vision of when slaves were sold on the pedestals and of the time they were getting right off the train, the railroad. He said, "Son, slaves was sold there and now you're here." He pointed at me and said, "You have a responsibility. You have a responsibility." I immediately connected with this gentleman. Tears started to flow down my face.

I said, "Thank you sir, I really appreciate those words."

He walked away and kept saying, "You have a responsibility! You have a responsibility!"

My heart was so happy, filled with joy, and part

sadness of what happened to my ancestors but knowing at that moment I was the chosen one to make a change. I knew then that Jirani Coffeehouse would be there forever. I knew that the vision I received was special. To this day, three years later, I have never seen this man again.

When you have an inspired business, people show up in your life. You don't have to know them, they're going to be total strangers, but they are assigned to you to give you words of encouragement and knowledge to continue and to connect you to the next phase of your vision.

DREAM REFLECTIONS

"You Have a Responsibility."

1. What did I take away from this chapter? What was the author's key message?

    _____

    _____

    _____

    _____

2. How does the author's story relate to my own personal story?

    _____

    _____

    _____

    _____

3. What is your WHY? What is the driving force behind your dream?

    _____

    _____

    _____

    _____

4. **What action am I going to take to apply the information I just read?**

_____

_____

_____

_____

COFFEE FACT

Espresso is weaker than regular coffee.

Don't let the price fool you—you'll need three shots of espresso to match the caffeine you get in one single, humble, regular cup of coffee.

CHAPTER NINE
RECURRING DREAMS

So the build-out was complete. We were fully staffed. We had a grand opening, and it was successful. Now it was on. We were open every day, and it was amazing. We stuck to our business plan and we had done cost projections to make sure we would have enough capital for the next eight months. We were expecting a slow growth, steady growth, one that we could keep up with. But that wasn't the case. This place blew up immediately. The first month we sold 5,000 pastries and 7,000 cups of coffee.

We weren't ready for this type of success. We immediately had to start buying more refrigerators, more equipment. The in-house bakers were working overnight trying to keep up with the demand. (By the way, they were the best pastries on the East Coast.)

"My number one lessons learned is when you have an inspired business, you must plan for ultimate success immediately."

I was caught off guard. These were things I called good problems. We had to recover quickly to keep up with this train. Ironically, we were located at the train tracks.

After a few months, the word got out. The media started coming from everywhere. We were featured in *USA Today* twice for businesses that support their community. Local news stations and newspapers and magazines started featuring us. They wanted to hear the story. They wanted to figure out how was I able to get the community in one place, living, eating, doing art together, enjoying coffee and tea. It was everyone's dream. If you came inside the Jirani Coffeehouse, at any time for any reason, you would immediately understand why our mission statement is *love*.

I was at the gym one day, and I got a call from one of the shift leaders, saying, "Ken, the governor is here." I couldn't understand what she was saying. I was trying to figure it out.

I said, "What did you say?"

She said, "The governor is here."

I looked down at myself. I had on basketball shorts and a tank top. So I immediately called my wife.

"Hey, the governor is in the shop. Can you go by there?"

She was on her way out of town, but I could not miss this opportunity. I did not know why or how the governor showed up in the shop, but I was going to meet the governor.

I quickly jumped into the car, rushed over to the shop. I got there, and it was true, the governor of Virginia was sitting having coffee with his staff, the secret service, and the first lady. I was honored. So, what do I do? I told him the story, and immediately his staff filmed me and him, and I was the small business spotlight. Oh, I couldn't believe that we were now being recognized throughout the state of Virginia.

You have to follow your dream. It's always bigger than what you initially can see. The more you believe the more you will be able to see.

This was such an exciting time. I was meeting new people, totally immersing myself into the community, and into the arts. I was in my special place. But no one really knew that behind the smile, I was having some anxiety about dealing with my mother's death. I was coming up on that first anniversary of her death, and I was nervous about it. I couldn't shake it. I tried to take time away.

I noticed, wherever I went, that people knew me. That was a little spooky to me. Anywhere I went in town, someone knew who I was. Then it started happening when I would go into the city. People would say, "There's the coffee house guy." My vision was much larger than me at this point.

I knew I still had to deal with my mother's death because I hadn't taken the time for myself. We were moving at such a rapid pace, I didn't know when I would have time for myself to deal with this. At this point, I hadn't visited my mother's grave and I knew after one year, I was going to have to do that to start the grieving process. Everyone knew and supported me.

I jumped on the road, headed back to Pennsylvania, got to my mother's grave alone. It was a special time. I knew this was the beginning of the healing process. I did not know that it would be another year later before it would really come down on me.

The contrast in my life was incredible. One side booming business, loving on community, walking in my purpose, walking in my passion. On the other side, I'm getting ready to have the first holiday season without my mother.

We were deep into the holiday season, coming up on Thanksgiving. I was back at the shop, it was thriving, families from all backgrounds were sitting inside of the shop taking advantage of all of the programs and events that were held in the shop. It was beautiful. Local high school choirs started to contact us because they needed a place to go to do holiday music and to also love on their community and they knew that Jirani coffeehouse was *the* place.

My siblings and I decided to have Thanksgiving together since this was the first year without our mother present. I remember going over to my brother's house. It was an awesome feeling to be around family and some friends. My oldest son Chuck was twenty-one at the time. He came in and remember thinking to myself how he had really been maturing and growing into a beautiful man. For some reason, that Thanksgiving I looked him in the eye and noticed just how beautiful he was. There was a glow about him that I just could not explain. His facial hair was well groomed, rich and he looked so healthy. His skin was flawless. He was dressed so well. Everyone just loved him. He outshone everyone in the room and I just enjoyed being in his presence.

For the first time in many years, when I think about all the years I had done retail, I was unable to enjoy a Thanksgiving with family while working in the retail business. As a retail executive, I went five years not being able to spend time with family during the holidays. There was always the Black Friday rush and then there was the Christmas rush. I could come and only stay for an hour. But once you have your own business, it's different.

The attraction of owning your own business is the true desire to have full control of your schedule. This is what I had for the first time in my life. I controlled my schedule.

I knew that I now could spend time with my friends and family the way I wanted to during the holidays. This was extra special. Now, being an entrepreneur full time, this was a gift to me. One of the main reasons that I desired to be an entrepreneur is because I wanted to give my children more life option: options to work for the family business, options to go to school and then return and add what you've learned to your family business. I knew that I could no longer continue to tell them to go after their dreams and not go after mine. Your children need to see a tangible example of what it looks like to actually go after your dreams.

I knew I had to be the one to lead them and open up

their minds to new possibilities. The Christmas season was amazing. For the first time in a long time I wasn't exhausted. The shop was doing great, and I was meeting more people in the community. I remember Christmas morning opening presents. My oldest son was with his mother, visiting her. We normally get the morning call. He called, greeted everyone, wished us well. We really missed him, but we were scheduled to meet him and spend time with him for New Year's.

I remember vividly, later on Christmas evening, I had my usual sweet potato pie, a nice drink, gifts were open, everyone was relaxing and then we actually dozed off early on Christmas night. But then I was awakened by a call from his mother. At the same time, I started receiving all these different texts: *Give me a call, give me a call.* I was thinking, what could have happened to my son? What did my son do? I was thinking there was a problem between him and his girlfriend. I wasn't sure. The phone rang again. It was his mother.

I picked up. To this day, the sound of her voice, her tone, will never leave me. "Ken, there's been an accident. We're at the emergency room now. They are working on Chuck. It's pretty serious, but they won't give me any information."

I had such a hard time trying to comprehend what she had just told me.

Okay, my son's in the hospital, there's been a car accident, you're there, they're working on him, they won't talk to you.

"What happened? What's going on?"

"I really don't know what's going on," she said. "But Chuck's in the hospital. There's been an accident."

Then all of the sudden, she said, "I got to go, they're here."

All I heard next was that dreaded click of a call ending too soon and then... *silence.*

I looked up and saw my daughter, my son, and my wife looking at me with a combination of puzzlement and worry spread over their faces. I said quietly, "Hey guys, Chuck was in an accident. I'm trying to find out what's going on."

I started to think, who would know if Chuck was having a problem? Who would be there? Who else is important enough in Chuck's life that would be at the hospital no matter what? Then it dawned on me. His cousin. These guys have been through thick and thin. They have been by each other's sides since they were babies and knew I could call him.

I gave his cousin a call. "Hey," I said. "What's going on? Are you at the hospital?"

At that moment, I received the worst news I have ever received in my life. My nephew screamed out to me over the phone.

"Uncle Chuck, he's gone. Uncle Chuck, he's gone."

Immediately, it felt like someone shoved an ice pick through my heart. I couldn't understand or comprehend what he just told me.

"Uncle Chuck, he's gone. He's gone."

All I remember is just yelling at the top of my lungs.

The days leading up to my son's funeral were hard. That week prior was a really tough time. I felt like my car broke down in the desert. No one was in sight, and I was walking on a two-lane highway with long, hot days.

The night time in the desert was freezing cold, no relief, no one in sight, all alone. This was a tough time. During this time I went through all the array of emotions that you can imagine. I started to think, here I am, dedicating my life to loving people. I know I'm called to love people, but with the same token, I lost two of the most important people in my life in such a short time. In 2015, I lost my mother, 2016, I lose my oldest son, and I had lost my father years prior, in 2009.

I knew that from this moment forward, I was forever changed. I would operate differently, I would think differently, I would love differently—still in a positive way, but this was tough. The amazing thing, as dark as this was, with all that was going on, with all these emotions, there still was the dream.

The dream was present in my life. When I was at a point where I was ready to give up, the dream was saying, what about me? What about the people that need me? I went back and forth with this, like, how can I deal with this dream when I'm dealing with a family crisis?

I have people I need to be strong for. I'm trying to be strong for myself, and now you're calling on me to tend to you, the dream. I almost started to resent the dream, because before the dream my life appeared to be "perfect." I had no problems. I didn't need to do this dream. Since pursuing this dream, all I had inherited were family issues. You just feel like you're under attack. "Why must I do with this dream? Why are you trying to take over my whole life?" is what I would say to the dream, but the dream would come with a sense of peace saying, I'm here, what about the people? I'm bigger than you. It's not about you.

I was overwhelmed emotionally. I knew I had to just accept the dream and its presence in my life, put it to the side and deal with this grief for my family and for myself. I knew I had to get through this.

In earlier chapters, I mentioned that one of the first things that God had to prepare me for was to get me in a position to receive. Once I received and accepted the dream, I had opened up a door without knowing I would now be in a position to receive an abundance of love from people that I didn't even know. When people heard what happened in my family, the floodgates of love poured out. I couldn't believe it. It was overwhelming.

From my church family, community, it was amazing. I mean, I would see people in the community that I didn't even know that had been watching me on social media, watching me live out this dream, doing the things that they didn't have the courage to do. They would walk up to me, tear filled eyes, hugging me, encouraging me, and at that moment it was so clear that we are on earth not to live alone, we cannot make it without each other. Without all of that love that my family received, there is no way we could have made it through such a tragic time. Humans need humans.

When I arrived at my son's funeral, to my surprise there were over 1,000 people there. I've never seen so many millennials in one place at one time, outside of a college campus. This place was flooded. People took buses to see this guy, to pay their respects for him. He touched so many lives in such a short period of time. It was obvious to me that his time, his job was done here on earth, I just had to accept the new way our relationship would be going forward until we met again.

Question to self: How do you live going forward? How do you live feeling like you don't have a lung, you're missing a kidney, and you have a huge part of your heart that's malfunctioning? How do you live going forward, knowing you're called to love, knowing that you have this dream that the community definitely needs? How are you going to live when you're in a state of wanting to be alone?

These were the questions that would continuously go through my mind. What many people don't know is that after my son's passing, I spent the first two months in my basement alone. I totally hid from everyone. For some reason, that basement was my comfort space. The four walls, nothing could get in and nothing could get out. I felt protected.

However, I had to realize I also have a mind that was free and I couldn't hide from the thoughts and all the people speaking to me during that dark time. All of the visions of love and the smiles from each person I had ever encountered and all of the encouraging words I'd ever heard would come to mind. And if you really listen, this is what is designed to help us get through these tough times. It's these dreams and visions that we're connected to.

They are there to pull us through. You need something bigger than yourself to help you get through tragic moments like this. I knew it was my time.

After spending many days in the basement, I woke up one morning at 7 AM and the first thing I heard was it's done. "It's done! Know that I didn't do this to you; I did this for him because he is with me now." I kept hearing those words over and over it's done! It's done! Then I realized that it's done meant that I was done with the deep, dark part of the grieving process. It's not that I felt any better or lighter. I just knew that I was DONE with this dark part of the process. I knew that I did not have to run from people anymore. I could stop hiding in my basement in the dark for hours. I could stop hiding from the fact and the reality. My beautiful, talented, wonderful son... was gone!

DREAM REFLECTIONS

"Dreams are not free. You have to count the cost."

1. What did I take away from this chapter? What
    was the author's key message?

    _____

    _____

    _____

    _____

2. How does the author's story relate to my own
    personal story?

    _____

    _____

    _____

    _____

3. Am I prepared for immediate success? If yes,
    is it written into my business plan?

    _____

    _____

    _____

    _____

4. **What action am I going to take to apply the information I just read?**

_____

_____

_____

_____

COFFEE FACT

Coffee stays warm longer when you add cream.

It seems to defy all known laws of thermodynamics, but adding cream to your coffee actually keeps it warm for 20% longer than keeping it black. It is truly a miracle wrought by a secret agreement between the coffee gods and the cream gods.

CHAPTER TEN
DREAM UNDERSTOOD

I know that at first read my entrepreneurial journey appears to be extremely heavy and challenging, but don't be discouraged. Not only is there a light at the end of the tunnel, but the light is always available to you along your journey.

Turn on the light!

So, let's pull this plane up 50,000 feet and fly above the clouds. As far as I can see, the skies are a magical blue, and the sun is so bright I have to wear my shades to enjoy such beauty. That is how I feel after surviving the peaks and valleys of life. I see life through new lenses because of my experiences. My peripheral vision is now 360 degrees, and I walk with a confidence that could not have been obtained without experiencing all of the wins and "losses." My cousin always talks about the law of relativity and I get it now.

We don't lose, we only learn and win.

Open your eyes and put on your new lenses and look around. Because of your experiences, you are equipped to handle any new challenge that may arise as you pursue your dreams. Don't ignore the voice inside of you that constantly reminds you that you didn't go through all of that hurt, pain, disappointment, struggle, fatigue, and trauma for nothing.

Believe the voice inside because what you've learned through it all has given you the tools and skills and insights you'll need in the next phase of your journey. Life, and all it brings us, is really about the push through challenges and about never giving up on the vision that you see daily while you are asleep and awake. You, too, can inhale and exhale the freshness of life after a tragedy.

I am now unstoppable, unshakeable, unbreakable, unmovable, and more importantly, I am unafraid!

The world is now my canvas, and I paint what I'm inspired to create. I get to choose whatever shapes, colors, and images I want to use on my canvas. There is a transfer of power to self when you know and trust that when you are in a fire, you will not get burned. Yes, the fire is hot, but I cannot be consumed by the fire.

There are at least 51 Bible verses that talk about God's "refining fire" and how it purifies us. This special kind of heavenly fire, whether it's financial, health, or a loss of loved ones, is designed not to destroy us, but to strengthen us.

Remember Job in the Old Testament? He loses all of his children, all of his livestock, all of his property, and all but one of his servants—all in the space of a few days! Then he's covered in boils! His friends are sure he's sinned. So they tell him to curse God, and yet he doesn't.

He knows he's in God's fire.

He says: *(Job 23:10) "But he knows the way that I take; when he has tried me, I shall come out as gold."*

I couldn't understand how we can be in the fire, but not consumed by it until someone explained to me that fire is what gold and silversmiths use to burn out the impurities in precious metals. Once the metal is heated the impurities rise to the top and are skimmed off, leaving just pure gold or silver.

Those precious metals have to be burned to be purified. Throughout the Bible, God takes his prophets and servants and puts them in situations that could only be defined as "crucibles" or fires. And in every instance they are in the fire, they are refined to prepare them for a major difference that's about to take place in their lives. Sometimes the tests come back-to-back, or close to one another, as mine did. Sometimes they are scattered throughout our lives. But they are designed to create "Christlikeness."

When King Nebuchadnezzar threw Shadrach, Meshach, and Abednego in the fire, they were not burned. But when the King looked into the furnace, he saw a fourth man there. When he asked them who the fourth man was, they told him, "Our God whom we serve. If He is able to deliver us from the burning fiery furnace, he will deliver us out of your hand, O King." And God did deliver them because of their faith.

Allow the fires in your life to burn, knowing they are not destroying you, but purifying you!

When I look back on the first year after my son's death, I see that year was the year of survival for me. I was figuring out how to live with this tragedy and how to walk out my dream and vision with this tragedy on my heart. It was just amazing, the people, and the community, how they would come out and share how they were just so encouraged, basically saying, "If you can do this, and experience that, I know I can accomplish my dream."

It is a special moment when you start to realize that your dream is connected to other people's dreams.

That's when the dream becomes bigger than yourself. That's when you don't feel like doing something, or a situation is not right, you find ways to execute your dream.

Now that Jirani Coffeehouse has been open for three years, I realized that it's one thing to follow your dream and open your business. It's another thing to maintain it. Within that first year, I saw so many businesses open and close their doors. What I learned from what I saw happen to others is that you have to *really know your business*. To do this start and constantly continue refining your processes. If you don't have them in place, make that a priority. Then keep adding new and better processes. Look constantly at your vendors and turn them into your partners. Here you help them help you. Constantly also look at where you're spending money. Also monitor your waste in whatever type of business you have. This is important. I knew I had to keep my coffee house open for the community and for my family.

Despite all the trials and tribulations, Jirani Coffeehouse has won and continues to win awards. We've won community awards as well as awards in the arts. We have also continued to receive press coverage from local television and newspapers. The articles about us are constant. People are really attached to our vision – the dream.

After that first year of survival, the second year at the coffee house was my year to live. Today I'm now living my dream, doing good business, continuing to love on people, and increasing my platform.

———————

If you have a dream, know it's something you *have to* go after. Look around. Open your eyes. The resources you need are there. They are right around you. They might not come in the package that you would like for them to come, but they are useful and important resources. Seek them out. Just remember, the dream that you have inside of you is not just your dream, it's so others, too, can walk out into theirs.

In the beginning of this book, I talked about when the entrepreneurial seed was planted in me. As a young child, I knew I wanted to be a businessman. Throughout my life, I've had many different jobs, always feeling like it wasn't the right place. Or, I had jobs that I really didn't like, but I took them for the experience. Whatever it was, I was always working as hard as if it were my dream job. I was always achieving and desiring to go to the next level. I think it's like the pros always say: "Practice like you play." If you practice at half-speed, you'll play at half-speed.

Don't be that guy or gal. When my dream finally arrived I didn't have to "up my game." I was used to working hard. If you put your best effort into whatever you're doing, whether you're stocking shelves, or cleaning bathrooms, God sees you, and so do others. People notice what you're doing even if you think they don't. Work and love like someone is always watching, because they are.

These were just different processes that the entrepreneurial seed had to go through to get me to the place where I am today. It wasn't easy. If it was easy, everyone would do it. Decide if you want the dream and are willing to chase it, or if you're content to just daydream and build castles in the air, but never really plan to live in them.

After many years of developing an array of skillsets, I was prepared and ready to receive when I heard the voice say "it's time to build a coffee house." At that point, I had no excuses. I knew that I was fully equipped to build anything and run any type of business from the ground up, if given the opportunity. My faith was in line. I knew that my life had prepared me for an opportunity like this. In my spirit I knew that nothing that had happened to me, good or bad, was wasted.

So, what seeds have been planted with inside of you? What wild and crazy business idea that keeps you up late at night, wrestles inside of your mind? It's the thing that just doesn't make sense. You probably don't have the money for it. It's the absolute wrong timing for you to do this dream. You might not feel equipped to do dream of that size. But for some reason, the thought, the images of you walking out this dream will not leave you. It keeps you up late at night and wakes you up early in the morning.

It is imperative that you identify the seed that has been planted within you. Once it's identified, then you must trust and accept that seed. Trust it in faith knowing that the things that you need will come on the other side of just accepting that this is the thing for you to do in this time of your life.

When I look back at my body of work, victories, trials and tribulations to my surprise I have been "making coffee" since I was a little boy. Food for thought: what are you making?

DREAM BIG!!

DREAM REFLECTIONS

What are you making with the ingredients of your life?

1. What did I take away from this chapter? What was the author's key message?

   _____

   _____

   _____

   _____

   _____

   _____

2. How does the author's story relate to my own personal story?

   _____

   _____

   _____

   _____

   _____

   _____

3. What action am I going to take to apply the

information I just read?

_____

_____

_____

_____

_____

_____

COFFEE FACT

Shepherds discovered coffee in Ethiopia circa 800 A.D.

Legend has it that 9th=century goat herders noticed the effect caffeine had on their goats, who appeared to "dance" after eating coffee berries. A local monk then made a drink with coffee berries and found that it kept him awake at night, thus the original cup of coffee was   born.

ABOUT THE AUTHOR

Ken Moorman is the visionary founder of the highly celebrated Jirani Coffeehouse located in Old Town Manassas, Virginia. Jirani is *The Place* for excellent coffee, conversations and a neighborhood hub for the arts and culture.

Ken's success with Jirani has been accompanied by his successful career as a Real Estate Agent in the Northern Virginia area for 14 years.

Ken grew up in a small town in the suburbs of North Philadelphia, PA called Bristol. After completing his term in the U.S. Army Ken was determined to live out his dream to be an entrepreneur.

Ken has a passion for community and the arts. In his spare time, he enjoys singing and helping others to achieve their dreams. He currently resides in Manassas Park, Virginia; with his wife, Detra and two children, Mabuto and Kendi.